Snow Leopards

EXPLORE
— my —
world

Jill Esbaum

NATIONAL
GEOGRAPHIC
KiDS

WASHINGTON, D.C.

A snow leopard!

She wanders rocky ridges, where sprouts push from unlikely cracks.

She crosses sun-dappled ravines, laps at trickles of melting snow, and explores dewy meadows buzzing with life.

What's she looking for?
A den. She finds a hidden
place, protected from icy
winds and swirling snow.

Here, she'll give birth
to two or three cubs.

Nuzzle

Mom stays close so the cubs know they're safe. Newborns are born with their eyes closed, too weak to move around much.

But, a week or so later . . . *Good morning, world!*

Special Cats

Most big cats have
yellow or gold eyes.
A snow leopard's eyes
are gray or pale green.

What color are *your* eyes?

African lion
Africa

Are you quiet or LOUD?

Do you have whiskers?

Most big cats roar. Snow leopards cannot. Instead, they growl, hiss, mew, moan, purr, and yowl. They also make a puffing sound called a chuff.

Can you hiss like a snow leopard?

mountain lion
North and South America

Pounce!

After two months in the den, cubs are ready to play! They roll and tumble and bat at each other.

By late summer, the cubs are following their mom everywhere, learning every nook and cranny of their rocky neighborhood.

Snow leopards like to be up high, where they can see a long way. *Ahhh . . .* a rocky outcropping is a great place to perch in the sun.

But if Mom sees a plump marmot, she's more than happy to chase it through tall grasses! Along a stream! Down a snowy slope! Her growing cubs need to eat.

What's for Lunch?

Do you eat meat?

Could you catch a bird?

Snow leopards are meat-eaters. They will feast on a wild sheep or goat for a week.

While hunting, is a snow leopard quiet or noisy?

Do you like green food?

Himalayan
blue sheep
India

Have you
ever walked
through snow?

Also on the menu are smaller
animals like marmots, pikas,
hares, and birds. Snow leopards
eat grass and twigs, too!

pika
China

golden marmot
India

Cold autumn nights turn mountain grasses dry and brittle. Wild sheep and goats move down the mountain for the winter.

Asiatic ibex
Central Asia

Snow leopards follow. Next year, the cubs will begin hunting. For now, as they watch Mom sneak after her prey, they are learning.

Blustery days? Freezing nights? Mountain winters are harsh.

Snow leopards must seek shelter from icy winds and howling blizzards.

Frosty Nights!

Extra thick fur keeps snow leopards warm. Long tails curl around to cover tender noses. *Nighty-night!*

What warms you on a cold night?

Are the tops of your ears round or pointy?

Small, rounded ears help hold in body heat.

Furry paws keep toes toasty.

Is your nose warm or cool?

23

Growl!

Vultures and ravens trying to steal a snow leopard's food soon find out that these cuddly-looking cats can be fierce fighters...

. . . especially if a mom thinks her cubs are in danger. Then watch out!

Cubs stay with their mom for nearly two years. She won't have more cubs until these are grown and gone.

When the young snow leopards are finally grown, they leave. Each must find a new neighborhood, or territory, to call its own.

Leap, snow leopard!

Live strong and free in your new hunting grounds.

Where Snow Leopards Live

Snow leopards live in the mountains
on the continent of Asia.

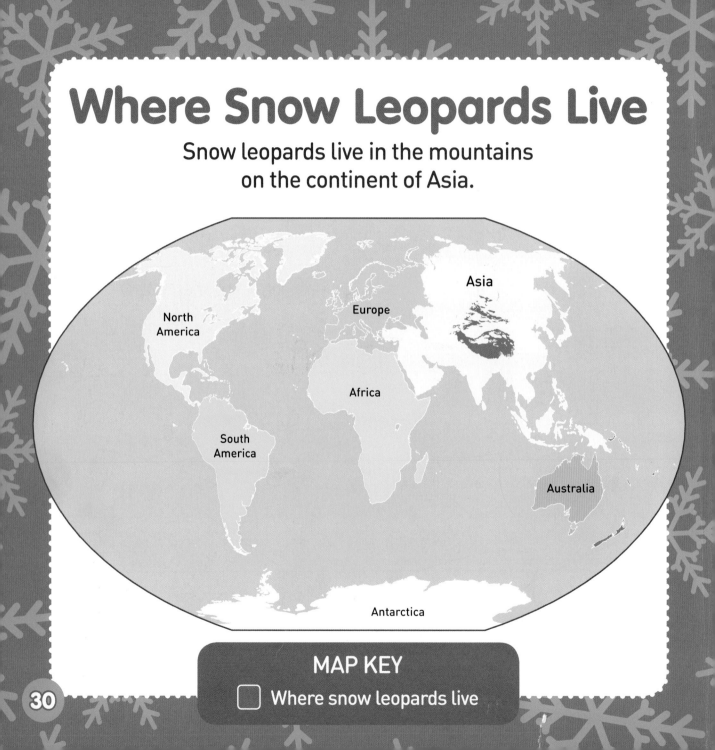

Asia

Europe

North
America

Africa

South
America

Australia

Antarctica

MAP KEY
☐ Where snow leopards live

Name the Parts of a Snow Leopard

Can you find all the parts of a snow leopard?

- paws
- tail
- eyes
- nose
- ears
- tummy

For Evelyn
—JE

Editor: Ariane Szu-Tu
Art Director: Amanda Larsen
Designer: Callie Broaddus
Photography Editor: Lori Epstein

National Geographic supports K-12 educators with
ELA Common Core Resources. Visit www.natgeoed.org/
commoncore for more information.

Trade paperback ISBN: 978-1-4263-1703-3

Reinforced library binding ISBN: 978-1-4263-1704-0

The publisher gratefully acknowledges Brad Rutherford,
executive director of the Snow Leopard Trust, and early
education expert Catherine Hughes for their expert review
of the book.

ILLUSTRATIONS CREDITS

*GI: Getty Images; MP: Minden Pictures; NGC: National
Geographic Creative; SS: Shutterstock*
Cover, Thomas Kitchin and Victoria Hurst/First Light/GI; back cover,
Lynn M. Stone/naturepl.com; 1, Mark Kolbe/GI; 2–3, imagebroker/
Alamy; 4–5, Daniel J. Cox/NaturalExposures.com; 6, Daniel J. Cox/
NaturalExposures.com; 7 (UP), Lisa and Mike Husar; 7 (LO), Ron
Kimball/Kimball Stock; 7, ivivankeulen/SS; 8, Daniel J. Cox/Natu-
ralExposures.com; 8, Maly Designer/SS; 9, Steve Bloom Images/
Alamy; 10 (LE), AccentAlaska.com/Alamy; 10 (UP), Victoria Hillman/
SS; 10 (LO), Laura Dyer/SS; 11 (UP), Peter Betts/SS; 11 (LOLE), M2
Photography/Alamy; 11 (LORT), Volodymyr Burdiak/SS; 12, Tom and
Pat Leeson; 13, Hideo Kurihara/Alamy; 13, ArtHeart/SS; 14, Tom and
Pat Leeson; 15 (UP), Cyril Ruoso/MP; 15, ylq/SS; 16 (LE), Dietmar Nill/
Foto Natura/MP; 16 (RT), Julian Rovagnati/SS; 17 (UPLE), Steve Win-
ter/NGC; 17 (UPRT), Design Pics Inc./Alamy; 17 (LOLE), FLPA/Alamy;
17 (LORT), Alex Treadway/NGC; 18, Barbara Saxa/AFP/GI; 19, Tom and
Pat Leeson; 20, Andy Rouse/naturepl.com; 21, Tim Fitzharris/MP; 22,
Daniel J. Cox/NaturalExposures.com; 23, Andy Rouse/naturepl.com;
23 (INSET), Lynn M. Stone/naturepl.com; 24, Don Johnston/All Can-
ada Photos/GI; 25, F1online digitale Bildagentur GmbH/Alamy; 26,
Eric Baccega/npl/MP; 27, Tom and Pat Leeson; 28–29, Tom and Pat
Leeson; 31, SuperStock/Alamy; 32, Juniors Bildarchiv GmbH/Alamy

Printed in the United States of America
14/WOR/1